Cut & Assemble
ICOSAHEDRA

Twelve Models in White and Color

EVE TORRENCE

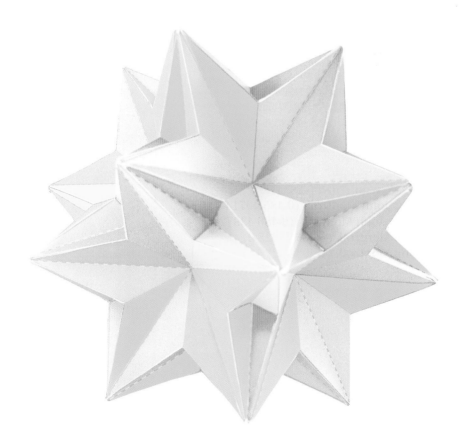

DOVER PUBLICATIONS, INC.
Mineola, New York

GREEN EDITION ®

At Dover Publications we're committed to producing books in an earth-friendly manner and to helping our customers make greener choices.

Manufacturing books in the United States ensures compliance with strict environmental laws and eliminates the need for international freight shipping, a major contributor to global air pollution. And printing on recycled paper helps minimize our consumption of trees, water and fossil fuels.

The text of this book was printed on paper made with 10% post-consumer waste and the cover was printed on paper made with 10% post-consumer waste. At Dover, we use Environmental Defense's Paper Calculator to measure the benefits of these choices, including: the number of trees saved, gallons of water conserved, as well as air emissions and solid waste eliminated.

Courier Corporation, the manufacturer of this book, owns the Green Edition Trademark.

Please visit the product page for *Cut & Assemble Icosahedra: Twelve Models in White and Color* at www.doverpublications.com to see a detailed account of the environmental savings we've achieved over the life of this book.

MATERIALS

- Pencil
- Small and large scissors
- X-ACTO knife
- Ruler
- White glue
- Small paintbrush
- Tweezers
- Toothpicks
- Straight pins

GENERAL DIRECTIONS

Caution: Children should always have adult supervision when using sharp objects. Numbers and letters that are printed outside the solid lines should be written on the adjacent triangles of the model in pencil *before* doing any cutting. Print very lightly so these marks can be easily erased when the model is complete. Cut out all models down the center of the thick solid lines using scissors or an X-ACTO knife. Use your ruler and X-ACTO knife to score the thin solid and dashed lines. All thin solid lines are mountain folds (fold paper away from yourself) and all thin dashed lines are valley folds (fold paper toward you). Use a small paintbrush to spread a thin layer of white glue on the tabs. Carefully glue one tab at a time. Hold each tab in place with your index finger and thumb until it is secure. Tweezers, toothpicks, and pins are helpful for holding the last few tabs in position for gluing.

Copyright

Copyright © 2011 by Eve Torrence
All rights reserved.

Bibliographical Note

Cut & Assemble Icosahedra: Twelve Models in White and Color is a new work, first published by Dover Publications, Inc., in 2011.

International Standard Book Number

ISBN-13: 978-0-486-48371-9
ISBN-10: 0-486-48371-1

Manufactured in the United States by Courier Corporation
48371101
www.doverpublications.com

The Icosahedron
Plate 1 (color & white)

Directions: Let's begin with the colored model. Cut out the piece down the center of the thick solid lines. Score along the thin solid lines. Make mountain folds along all the scored lines. Glue each of the white tabs marked with a minus sign (−) to the back of the adjacent colored triangle. It will be clear where to glue the last three tabs to form the solid model. Complete the white model in the same manner.

Geometry: The icosahedron is one of the five regular solids. These solids are very symmetric. All the flat surfaces (called the faces) are the same regular polygon. A polygon is called regular when all the angles have the same measurement and all the sides are the same length. For the icosahedron all the faces are equilateral triangles. The sides of the polygons are called edges and where two edges meet in a point is called a vertex. The other property of a regular solid is that the same number of faces meet at each vertex. On the icosahedron five triangles meet at each vertex.

There are only five solids that meet all these criteria. They are the tetrahedron (four equilateral triangles arranged with three triangles meeting at each vertex), the octahedron (eight equilateral triangles with four triangles meeting at each vertex), the icosahedron (twenty equilateral triangles with five triangles meeting at each vertex), the cube (six squares with three squares meeting at each vertex), and the dodecahedron (twelve pentagons with three pentagons meeting at each vertex). These five solids are also called the Platonic solids. The ancient Greeks knew there were only five possibilities for regular solids and they thought this was a surprising and delightful property of solid geometry.

The twenty faces of the icosahedron are colored with ten colors. Parallel faces are the same color. This coloring will be used to reveal how several other models are related to the icosahedron.

The First Stellation of the Icosahedron
Plate 2 (color), Plate 3 (white)

Directions: Use a pencil to write the letters outside the thick black lines on the adjacent colored triangles. Cut along the thick solid lines and score along the thin solid and dashed lines. Fold mountain and valley folds as marked. Glue each of the white tabs marked with a minus sign (−) to the back of the adjacent colored triangle. Next glue the lettered tabs to the back of the corresponding lettered triangles (see your pencil marks). Complete the four separate pieces before gluing them together. Save the small piece marked L, M, N for last. The white model is constructed in the same manner.

Geometry: Stellation is a process by which a very symmetric polyhedron (called a uniform polyhedron) can be formed from a Platonic solid. To understand this concept place the colored icosahedon with a yellow face in front. Imagine extending the planes of the three triangles adjacent to the yellow one. If you extended them until they met they would form a three-sided pyramid above the yellow triangle. Now look at the first stellation with a yellow face in front. Do you see the pyramid you imagined? See if you can match up the colors of the faces surrounding the yellow face of the icosahedron with the faces of the small pyramid. If it doesn't match, flip over the model to the other yellow face. If you extended all the faces of the icosahedron until they met, you would get twenty three-sided pyramids lying above the twenty faces of the icosahedron. The uniform polyhedron formed in this way is the first stellation of the icosahedron. Study your models to see how all the colors of the two models have the same arrangement.

The Compound of Five Octahedra
Plates 4–5 (color), Plates 6–7 (white)

Directions: Use a pencil to write the numbers outside the thick black lines on the adjacent colored triangles. Cut along the thick solid lines and score along the thin solid and dashed lines. Fold mountain and valley folds as marked. Glue each of the white tabs marked with a minus sign (−) to the back of the adjacent colored triangle. This will form many single colored four-sided pyramids. Next, glue numbered tabs to the back of the corresponding numbered triangles (see your pencil marks). Complete the six separate pieces before gluing them together. Save the smallest piece for last. The white model is constructed in the same manner.

Geometry: Recall that an octahedron has eight faces. Each face is an equilateral triangle and four triangles meet at each vertex. Look at just the yellow colored pieces while trying to ignore the rest of this model. They form an octahedron that intersects the rest of the model. Chose another color and examine just those pieces to find another octahedron. See if you can find all five octahedra.

The Second Stellation of the Icosahedron
Plates 8–9 (color)

Directions: This color model is constructed in the same manner as the compound of five octahedra (Plates 4–5).

Geometry: Line up the icosahedron, the first stellation, and the second stellation with a yellow face in the front of all three models. If you imagine extending the faces of first stellation until they meet they will form the four-sided pyramids of the second stellation. For example, examine the four sides of the first stellation that are colored light blue, green, dark blue, and orange. Imagine how, when extended, they will intersect and form the four-sided pyramid made of these four colors. Line up the first and second stellations so that the face colorings match. If they don't match, flip over one model to the other yellow face. Can you see how the second stellation is formed from the first stellation? The first stellation is made of twenty intersecting irregular hexagons in the same arrangement as the icosahedron. The second stellation is made of twenty intersecting irregular six-pointed stars in the same arrangement as the icosahedron. You'll notice the shapes are getting bigger. This is because they are all designed on the same scale. The second stellation is the size that would be formed if you extended the faces of the icosahedron model until they intersected the second time.

The Third Stellation of the Icosahedron
Plates 10–12 (white), Plates 13–15 (color)

Directions: Begin by cutting out the twelve identical pieces of the white model along the thick solid lines and scoring the thin solid and dashed lines. Fold mountain and valley folds as marked. Glue the tab marked with a minus sign (−) to the back of the adjacent dart shaped face on all twelve pieces. Gluing the pieces together is a little awkward.

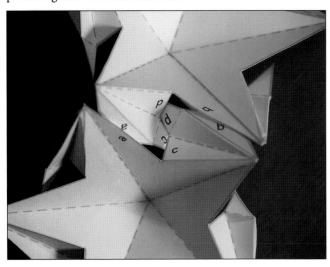

First glue the long thin tabs (a and b) under the dart-shaped faces. Then glue the triangular tabs (c and d) under the tall thin triangles that join the pieces. After gluing two pieces, join a third piece to both of these. Continue to add pieces in this configuration.

The twelve pieces on plates 13, 14, and 15 are constructed in the same manner. The tabs that are marked with the same letter or number are *not* glued to each other but are adjacent tabs.

Geometry: When the faces of the icosahedron are extended they intersect many times. They create many polygons that can be formed into uniform polyhedra. While it is easy to see how the first and second stellations are formed from the icosahedron, the third stellation is not as simple. Start with a yellow face in front and arrange the model so that the color arrangement matches the other models. The model is made of twenty identical faces that are in the same arrangement as the icosahedron. This model is on the same scale as the others. Can you imagine the icosahedron placed inside this model so that the vertices of the icosahedron meet the dimples in the centers of the twelve pieces of this model?

The Ten Intersecting Tetrahedra
Plates 16–18 (color)

Directions: This model is constructed in the same manner as the third stellation of the icosahedron (Plates 13–15).

Geometry: This model is colored to reveal that the third stellation of the icosahedron is also a compound of polyhedra. Look at the yellow parts of the model and try to ignore the rest of the model. Slowly turn the model to see that you have parts of four yellow equilateral triangles. These form a tetrahedron (a pyramid with a triangular base). Pick another color and find another tetrahedron. Can you find all ten?

The Fourth Stellation of the Icosahedron
Plates 19–24 (white), Plates 25–30 (color)

Directions: Begin with the white model to get a sense of how th pieces go together without having to worry about matchi tabs. Cut along thick solid lines, score and fold. Glue pairs adjacent tabs marked with plus signs (+) to each other on forty-two pieces. On the twelve large pieces glue the long th tab marked with a minus sign (−) under the adjacent face form a cone. The thirty small pieces join the twelve large piec together. Start by gluing five small pieces to one cone as show

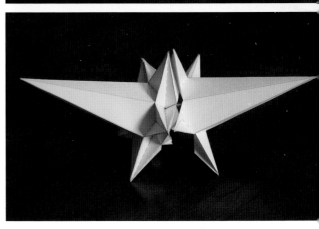

Then attach another cone to one of these small pieces and su round it with four more small pieces. Join a third co between the first two. Continue to add pieces to form a sy metric model.

Before beginning the colored model write the numbers th are outside the thick solid lines on the nearest colored triang The color model is then constructed in the same manner as t white model while gluing numbered tabs to the back of t corresponding pencil numbered triangles.

Geometry: This model is made up of twenty identically shap faces arranged and colored like the other stellations. Again t scale is the same as the other models. It can also be deriv from the third stellation by adding a cone to the center of ea dimple of that model.

This is far from the end of the story. There are fifty-eig unique stellations of the icosahedron. You have only just beg your explorations of these beautiful shapes.

ICOSAHEDRON — PLATE 1

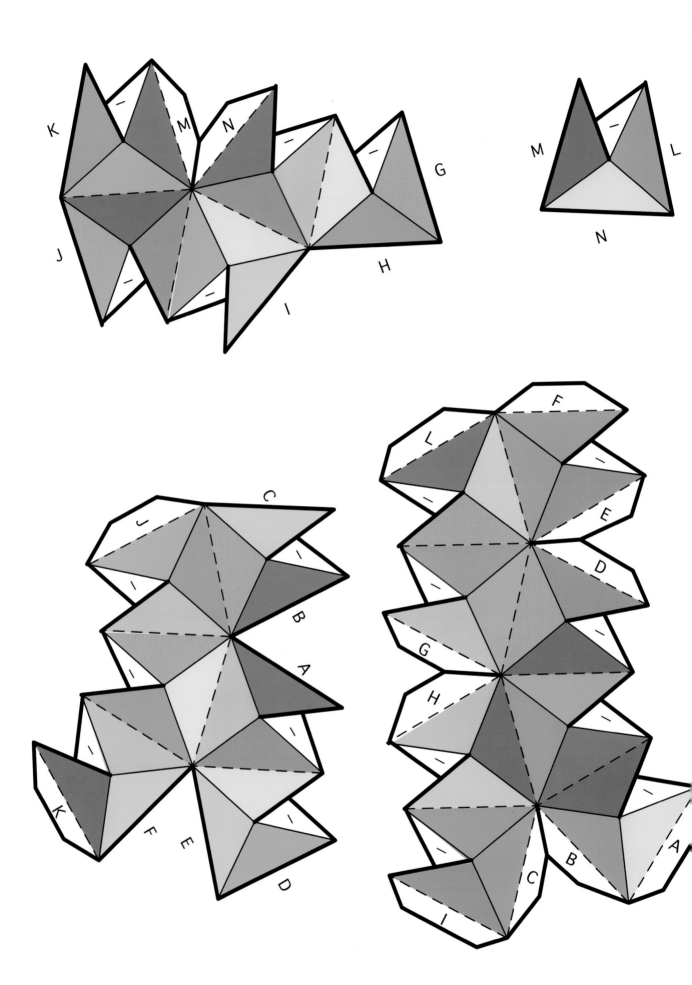

PLATE 2 — FIRST STELLATION OF THE ICOSAHEDRON

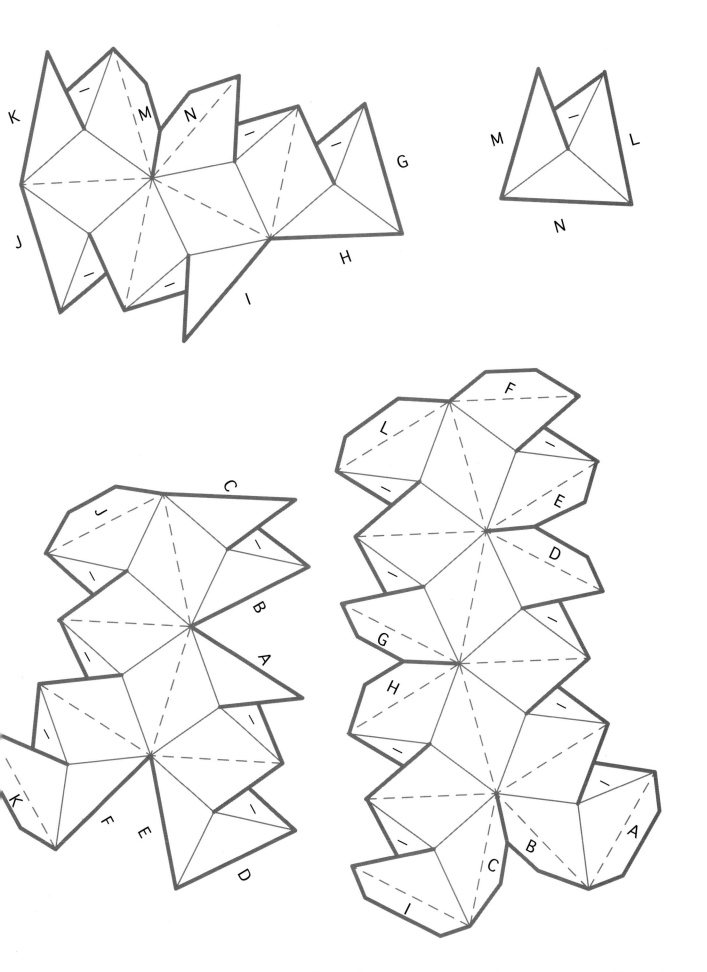

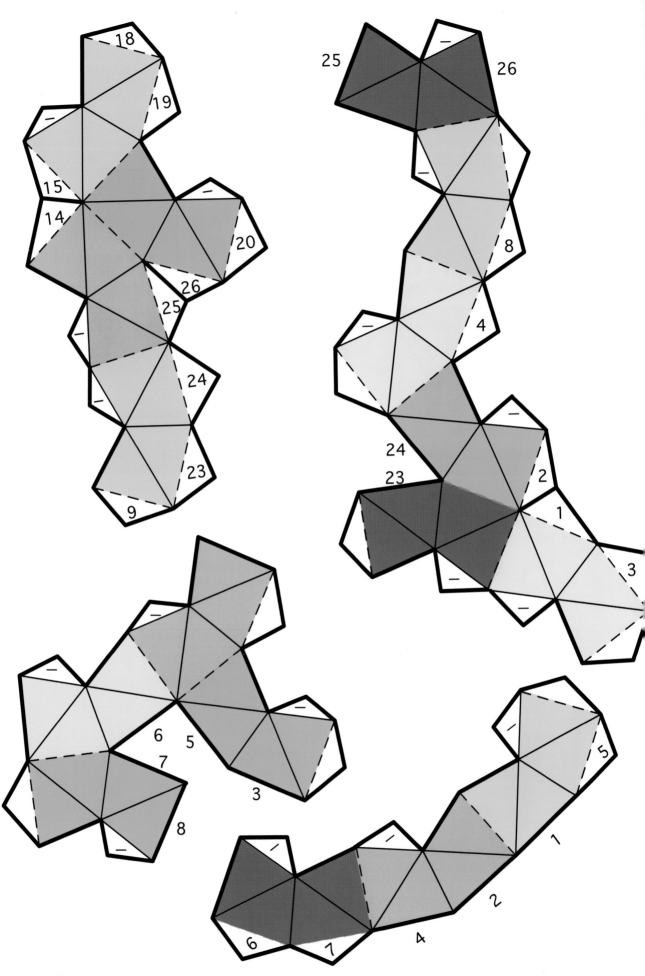

PLATE 4 — COMPOUND OF FIVE OCTAHEDRA

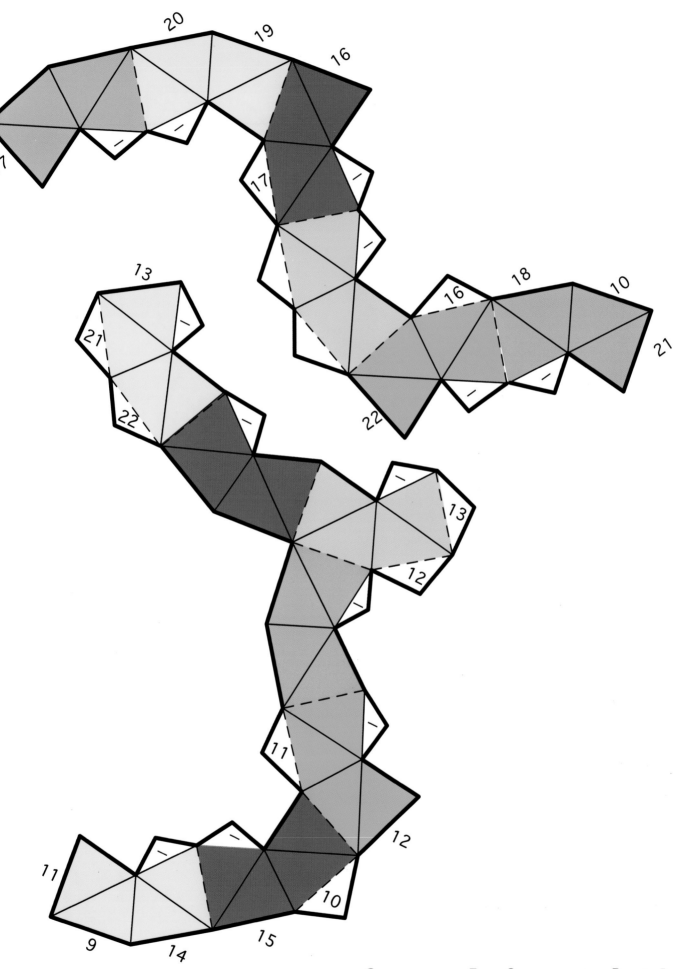

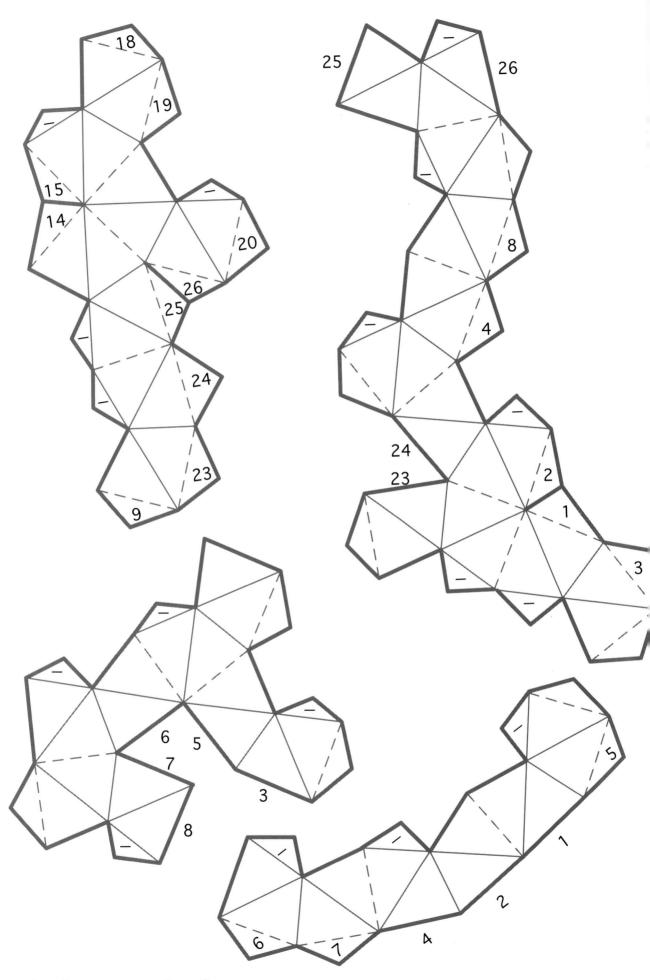

PLATE 6 — COMPOUND OF FIVE OCTAHEDRA

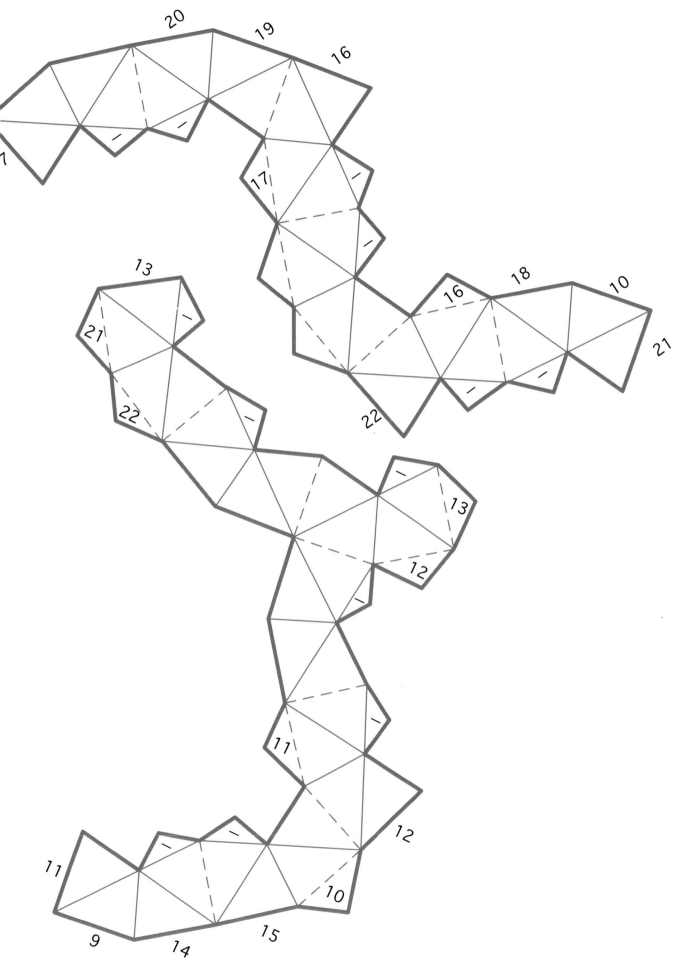

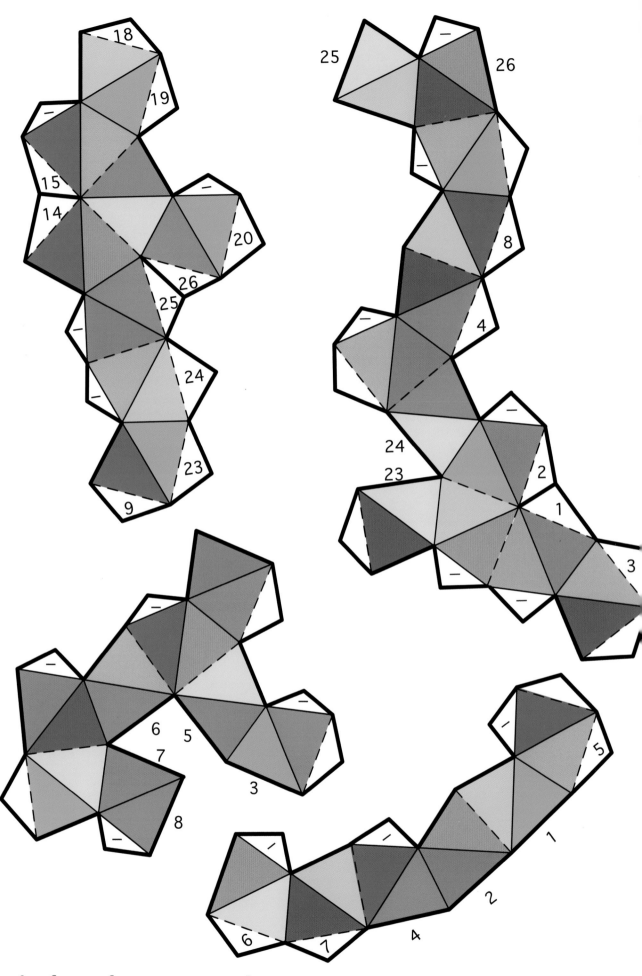

PLATE 8 — SECOND STELLATION OF THE ICOSAHEDRON

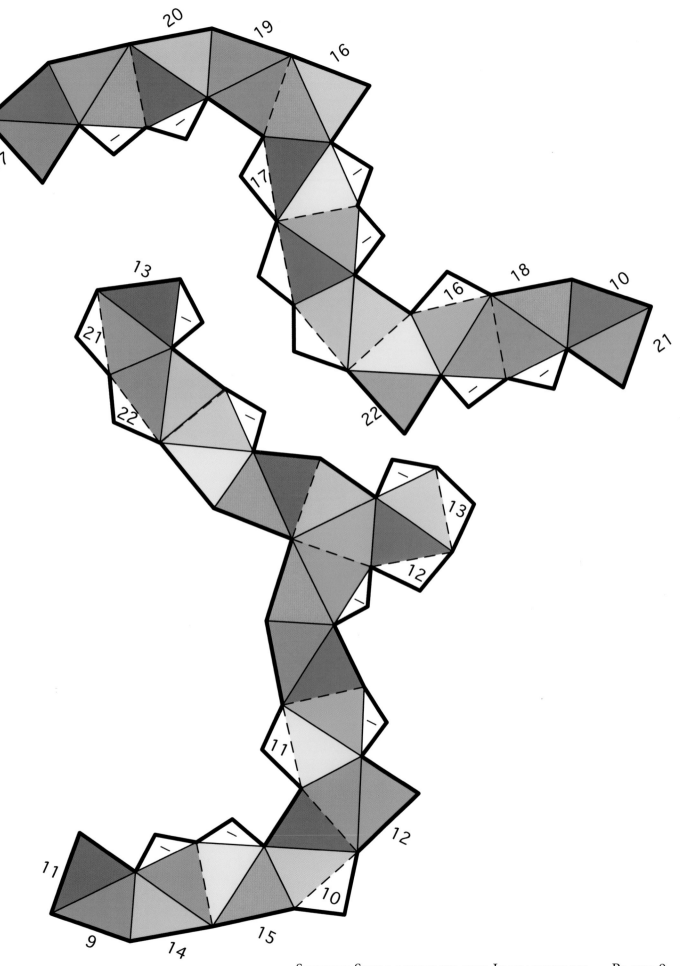

PLATE 10 — THIRD STELLATION OF THE ICOSAHEDRON

PLATE 12 — THIRD STELLATION OF THE ICOSAHEDRON

Plate 14 — Third Stellation of the Icosahedron

PLATE 16 — TEN INTERSECTING TETRAHEDRA

PLATE 18 — TEN INTERSECTING TETRAHEDRA

PLATE 20 — FOURTH STELLATION OF THE ICOSAHEDRON

PLATE 22 — FOURTH STELLATION OF THE ICOSAHEDRON

PLATE 24 — FOURTH STELLATION OF THE ICOSAHEDRON

PLATE 26 — FOURTH STELLATION OF THE ICOSAHEDRON

PLATE 28 — FOURTH STELLATION OF THE ICOSAHEDRON